Alpine Flower Designs
for Artists & Craftsmen

Color Plates by
François Gos

Black-and-White Plates by
Karen Baldauski

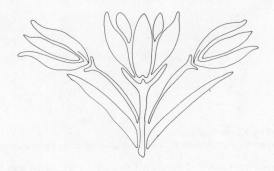

Dover Publications, Inc.
New York

Publisher's Note

Floral ornament was at the heart of Art Nouveau design. It was the growth patterns of plants and the curvilinear shapes of flowers that inspired the swirling, "organic" look of an art style that is still with us today.

Of the numerous color portfolios published at the turn of the century as models for artists, designers and craftsmen, one of the finest and rarest is the 20-plate *La Flore Alpine: Documents décoratifs* of 1903 by Francois-Marc-Eugène Gos. Born in Geneva in 1880 (a 1955 reference book implies that he was still alive at the time of writing), Gos became a painter like his father Albert and an author like his brother Charles. He studied painting in Geneva, Paris and Munich, and founded an art school in Lausanne. In three full-length books he described the Alpine regions of Switzerland and France with which he was so intimately acquainted: *Aux pays des Muverans (Les Alpes vaudoises)* (Lausanne, 1924), *Zermatt et sa vallée* (Geneva, 1925) and *Les Alpes de la Haute-Savoie* (Geneva, 1926). The latter two were published in English translation in London a year after their first appearance, as *Zermatt and Its Valley* and *Rambles in High Savoy*, respectively.

In *La Flore Alpine*, Gos devoted each plate to one flowering plant (one plate includes two closely related plants), which he presented in several panels in a variety of extremely useful designs and patterns. The present volume reproduces the 16 finest plates in full color. The English and scientific plant names that correspond to the French names in the original publication have been taken from *A Dictionary of Plant Names* by H. L. Gerth Van Wijk (published by Martinus Nijhoff, The Hague, 1909, 1910 and 1916; Vols. 1 and 2 reprinted by A. Asher & Co., Amsterdam, 1962).

A new and unusual feature of the present volume is the addition of black-and-white drawings by Karen Baldauski, who has taken 90 elements of the color plates (sometimes not a whole panel, but just a sprig or other detail) and has rendered them in contour line. Ms. Baldauski's drawings are not only immediately useful just as they stand for a wide variety of design and craft purposes, but are also object lessons in how to derive new art works from old.

Published in Canada by General Publishing Company, Ltd., 30 Lesmill Road, Don Mills, Toronto, Ontario.

Published in the United Kingdom by Constable and Company, Ltd., 10 Orange Street, London WC2H 7EG.

Alpine Flower Designs for Artists and Craftsmen is a new work, first published by Dover Publications, Inc., in 1980. The 16 color plates have been reproduced from the portfolio *La Flore Alpine: Documents décoratifs*, by F. Gos, originally published by the Librairie Centrale des Beaux-Arts, Paris, in 1903.

DOVER *Pictorial Archive* SERIES

International Standard Book Number: 0-486-23982-9
Library of Congress Catalog Card Number: 80-65450

Manufactured in the United States of America
Dover Publications, Inc.
180 Varick Street
New York, N.Y. 10014

Contents

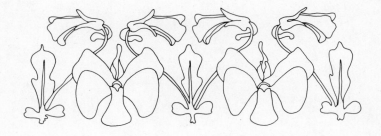

Rhododendron

Hare's-ear

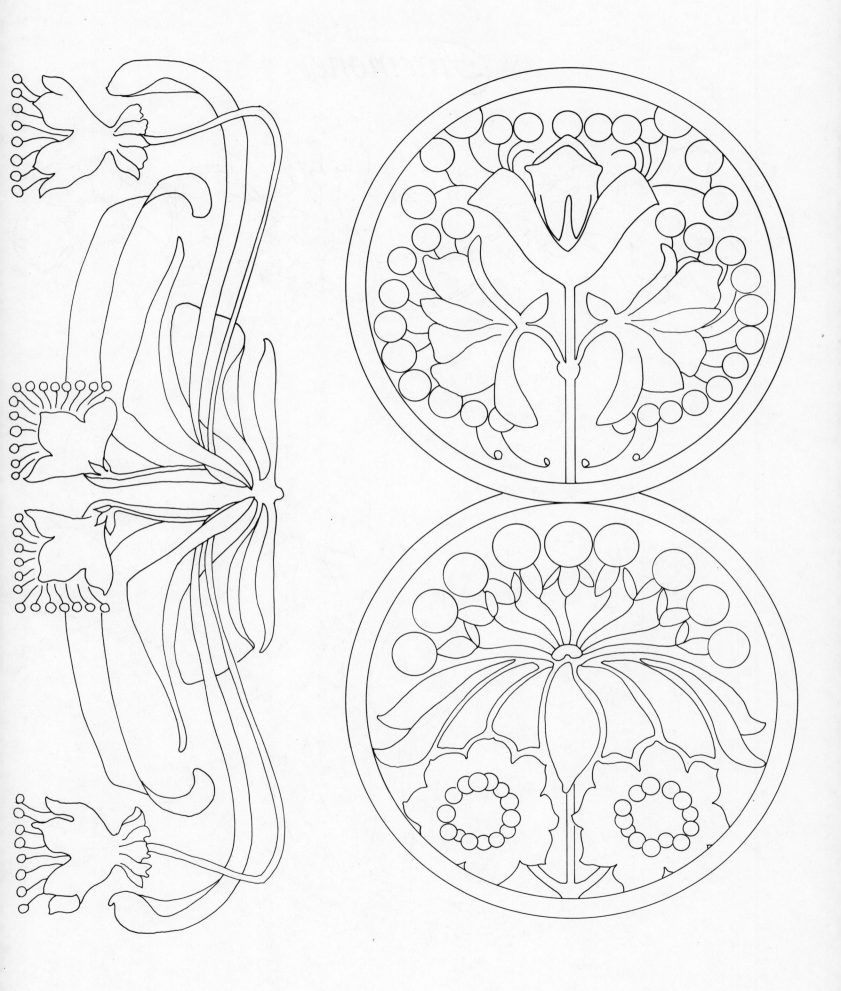

Anemone

Dogtooth Violet

Bearberry

Rhododendron

Plate I

Hare's-ear

PLATE II

Anemone

PLATE III

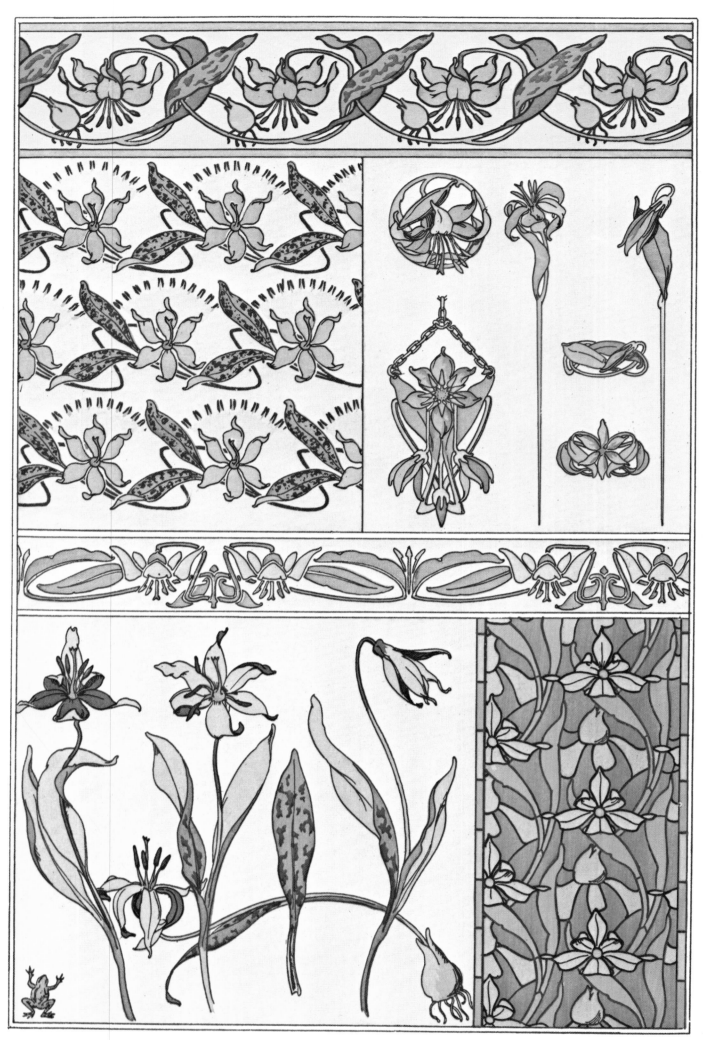

Dogtooth Violet

PLATE IV

Bearberry

PLATE V

Clammy Lychnis

PLATE VI

Viola

PLATE VII

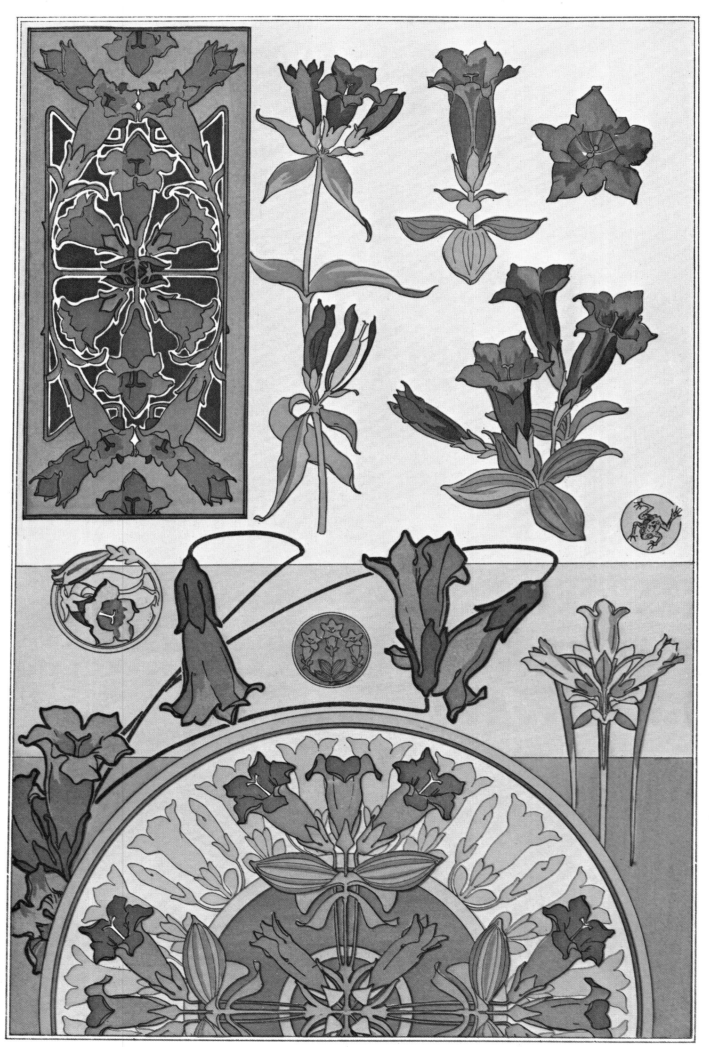

Purple Gentian and Gentianella

PLATE VIII

Arnica

Plate IX

Wood Pink

PLATE X

Yellow Gentian

PLATE XI

Mezereon

PLATE XII

Crocus

PLATE XIII

Hepatica

PLATE XIV

Rampion

PLATE XV

Alpine Soldanella

PLATE XVI

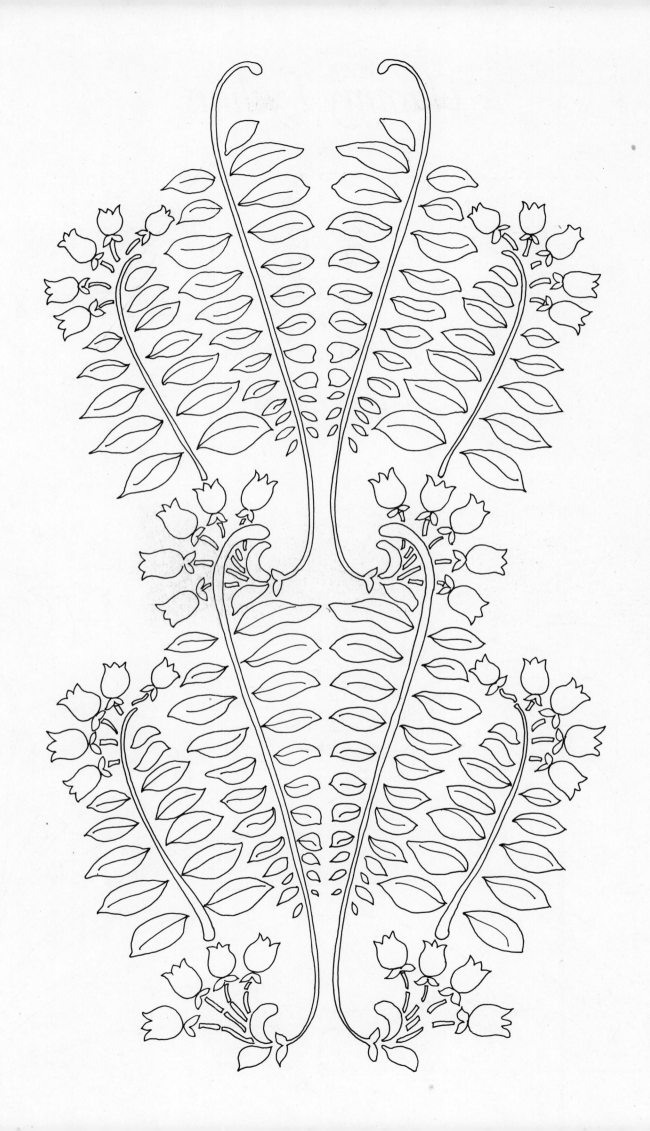

Clammy Lychnis

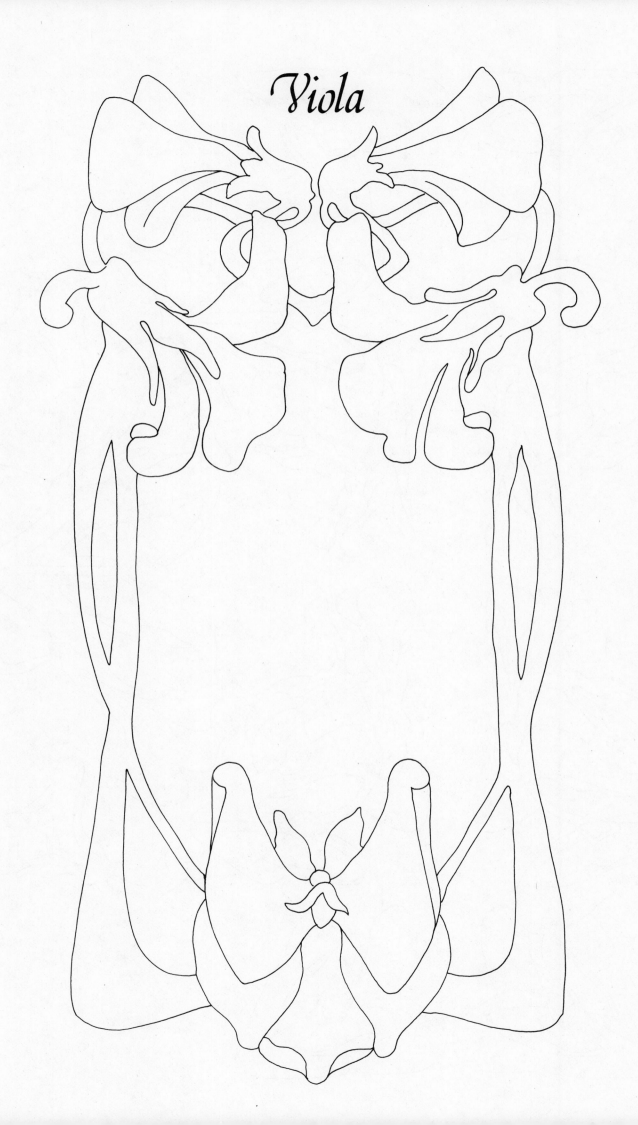

Viola

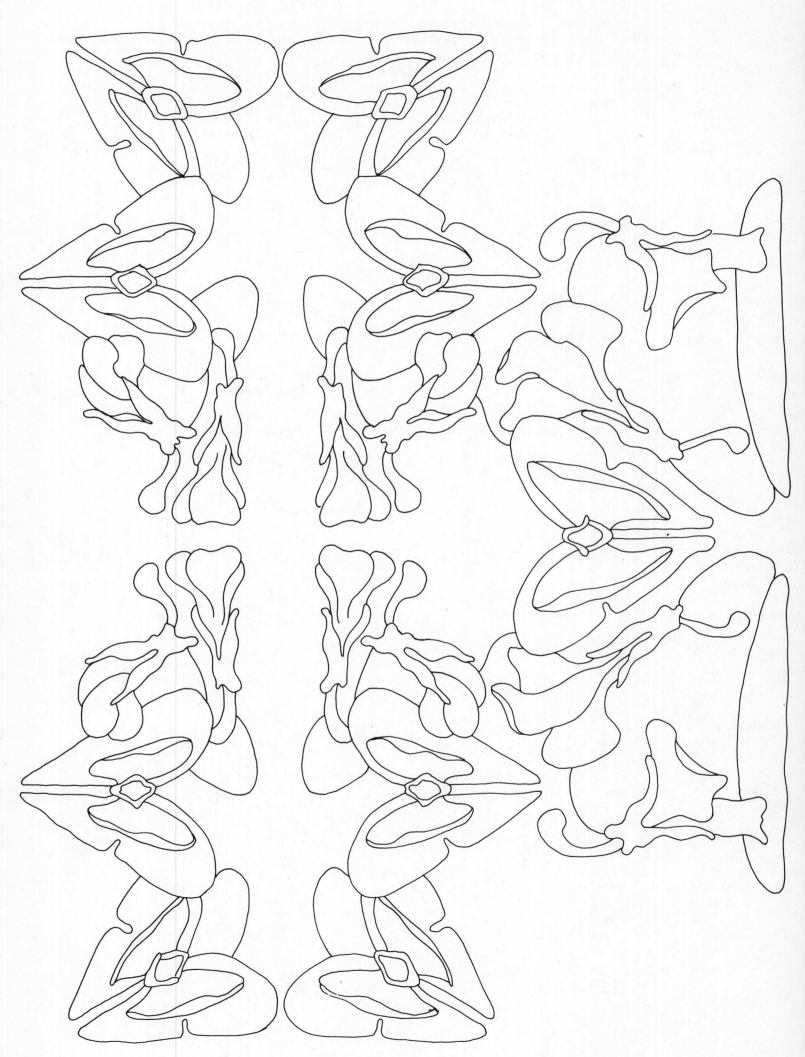

Purple Gentian and Gentianella

Arnica

Wood Pink

Yellow Gentian

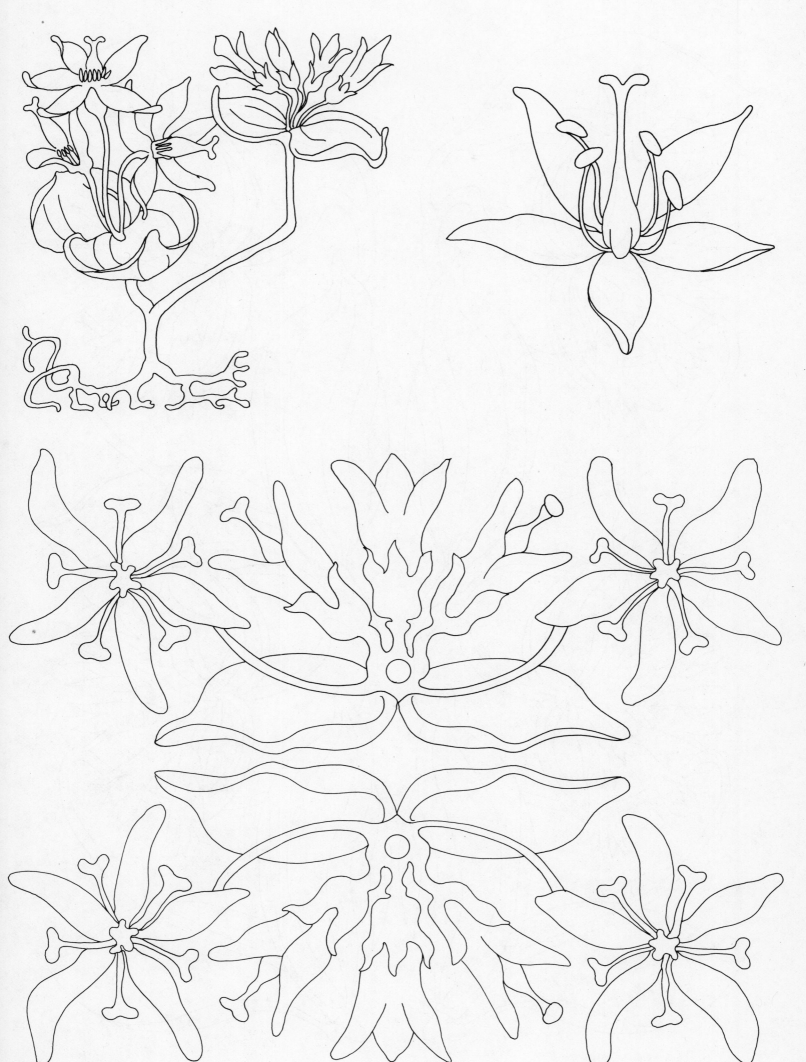

Mezereon

Crocus

Hepatica

Rampion

41

Alpine Soldanella

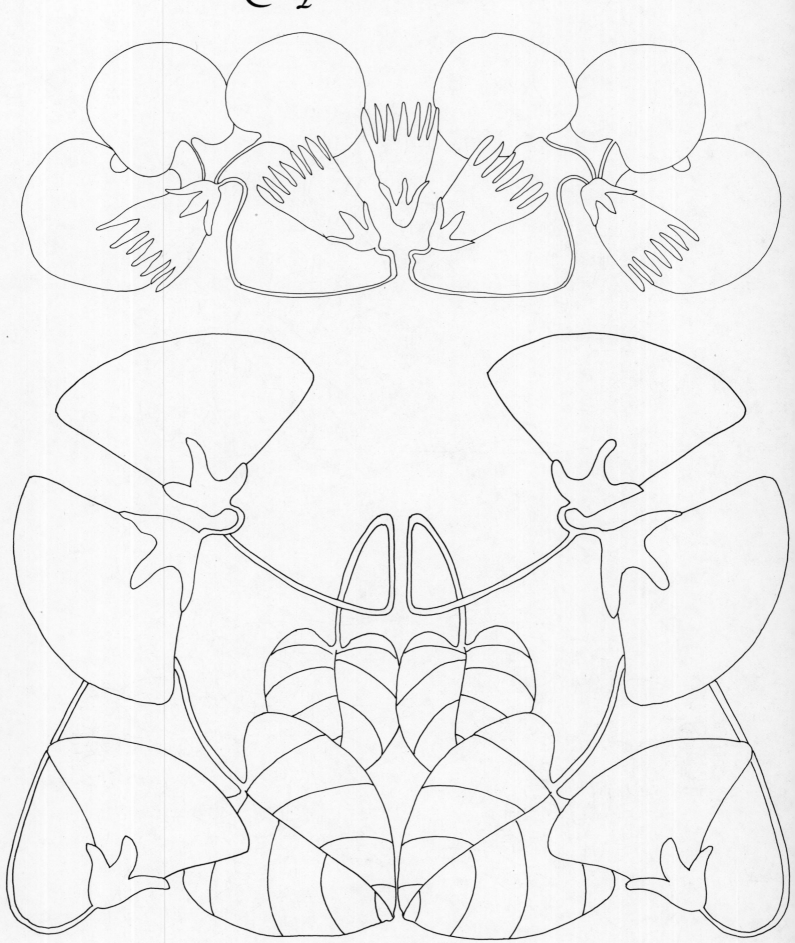

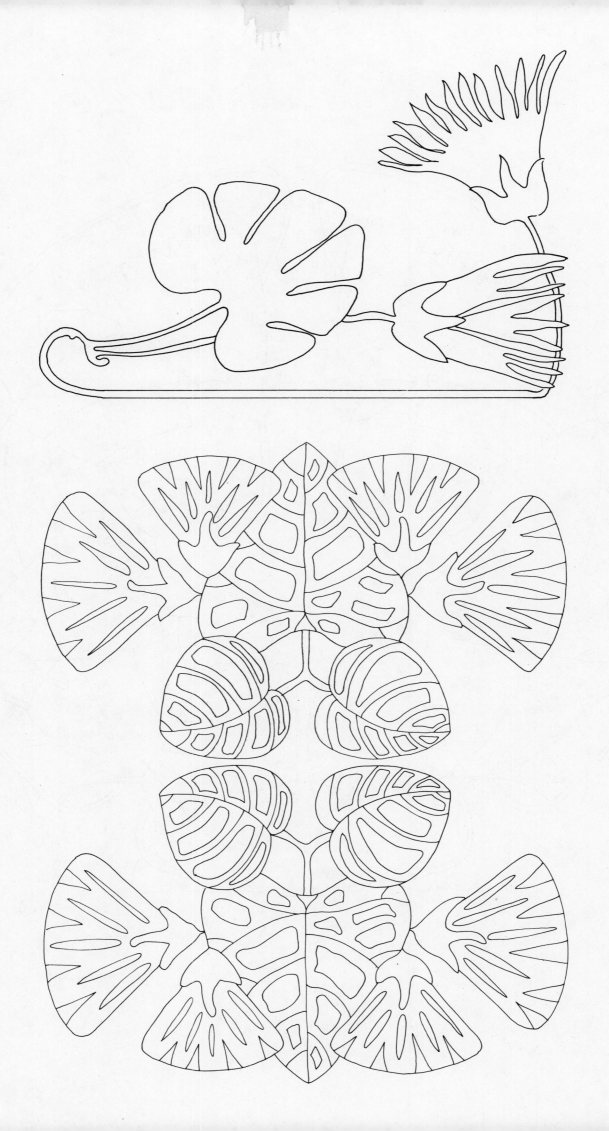